It's okay to be happy.

1

It's okay not to do anything on the weekends. That's what weekends are for.

It's okay to work on the weekends if that's what you want to do.

It's okay to be happy

by J.F. Mulholland

Illustrations by Alka Joshi

Tipperary Press
Stanford, California

Published by Tipperary Press, P.O. Box 9940, Stanford, California, 94309.

ISBN 1-884621-00-7

Printed in the United States of America
First Printing
10 9 8 7 6 5 4 3 2 1

...

I wrote this book for my sweetie. She was feeling down. She felt she needed permission to be happy. These little sayings perked her up so much, she wanted to do the illustrations.

As with any advice, you should take the advice in this book with a grain of salt.

J.F. Mulholland
Wisteria Lodge, 1994

...

It's okay to have fun.

It's okay to live in a small house when you're only 35.

It's okay to live in a small house when you're 90. No one will think the less of you.

It's okay to have friends who live in big houses. Friends don't care what kind of house you live in.

It's okay for friends to make more money than you.

It's okay to make less money than your friends. Money is good for buying things. Money does not define your quality of life. Even poor people can be happy.

It's okay to make mistakes.

It's okay for friends to make mistakes.

It's okay for friends to have faults.

It's okay not to like your friends' faults—that's why you have other friends.

It's okay to be nice.

It's okay to smile.

It's okay to have dessert.

It's okay to get mad at someone. You should try not to hurt their feelings. You should apologize if you hurt their feelings.

It's not okay to take out your anger on someone who is not responsible for it.

It's okay to fail.

It's okay to try again.

It's okay to fall when you're learning to walk. If you fall, just keep going.

It's okay to be smarter than other people. But you don't have to make sure they know it.

It's okay to apologize.

It's okay to be optimistic.

It's okay to take care of someone who needs your help.

It's okay to thank someone for helping you.

It's okay to set high goals. As Daniel Burnham said, make no small plans, for they have not the power to move men's minds.

It's okay to have strong ideas that nobody seems to like. As Einstein said, great spirits have often encountered violent opposition from mediocre minds.

It's okay to learn something new, no matter how old you are.

It's okay to be friendly.

It's okay to talk to people on the bus or waiting in line.

It's okay to lose your temper. Everyone does. Just be careful what you say and do. It's not okay to hurt people.

It's okay to forsake short-term pleasure for long-term gain.

It's okay to talk to the person next to you in the theater.

It's okay to be different.

It's okay to say no.

It's okay to like things that your friends don't like.

It's okay to get compliments.

It's okay to give compliments.

It's okay to encounter obstacles as you strive to reach a goal. Just find a way around them.

It's okay to loan a friend a little money. If you loan a lot of money, you may not have a friend anymore.

It's okay to borrow a little money from a friend. Be sure to pay it back promptly.

It's okay to be on welfare. It's not a crime to be poor.

It's okay to try to find a job to get off welfare.

It's okay to be rejected when you apply for a job. They're not rejecting you. They're rejecting the job application.

It's okay to be cut from a team. There will be many more chances to get on a team if you want to take them.

It's okay for a friend to get on a team even if you get cut.

It's okay to get on a team, even if a friend gets cut.

It's okay to be successful.

It's okay to set high standards.

It's okay to study or work when your friends want to play.

It's okay to feel unloved. You're probably not unloved.

It's okay to divide a big job into bite-sized tasks that you can accomplish one at a time.

It's okay to forgive others. It's okay to ask for forgiveness.

It's okay to plan for the future.

It's okay to stop and smell the roses.

It's okay to stop and smell
the plum blossoms, too.

It's okay not to worry. It's okay to worry.

It's okay to remember terrible things that have happened to you. If you remember them, then you know you survived them.

It's okay to dream.

It's okay to love someone unconditionally.

It's okay to ask dumb questions.

It's okay to ask smart questions.

It's okay to ask questions when you don't understand something.

It's okay to do other work when a meeting is boring. If it were a truly important meeting, it wouldn't be boring.

It's okay to doodle during meetings.

It's okay to give money to charities. They can do good things with your money when you don't have the time or ability to do those good things yourself.

It's okay not to give money to a charity if you have the time or ability to do good things yourself.

It's okay not to give money to a charity if you can't afford it.

It's okay to have a car with a leaky convertible top, seats that are falling apart, and a hole in the floor.

It's okay to wear hand-me-downs.

It's okay to give your old clothes to charity.

It's okay to buy clothes at a thrift shop.

It's okay to use coupons for purchases. That's what they're for.

It's okay to take longer than you expected to do something.

It's okay to get a project done ahead of the deadline.

It's okay to ask for an extension. Even the IRS gives extensions.

It's okay not to be perfect. Nobody's perfect.

It's okay to try to be perfect. But give yourself permission to fail.

It's okay to have something wrong with you. Everyone has something wrong with them.

It's okay not to change your own oil.

It's okay not to do home repairs yourself.

It's okay to tell your friends what you would really like to do tonight when they ask you what you'd like to do tonight.

It's okay to be turned down for a date. There really are plenty of fish in the sea. It's not worth making yourself miserable.

It's okay to be turned down when you ask someone to dance. Ask someone else.

It's okay to ask someone out that you have a crush on. They might actually go out with you.

It's okay to have a date where you don't have to spend a lot of money. Take a walk. Go to the park. Go window-shopping. It's still a date, and it's still fun.

It's okay to turn someone down for a date. Don't make up some excuse to be nice; just be honest and considerate.

It's okay to learn a foreign language. It's okay to learn your parents' language, too, even if people make fun of it.

It's okay for someone to have difficulty speaking English while they are still learning the language. You don't expect babies to speak perfectly.

It's okay for people to have different skin colors and differently shaped eyes.

It's okay to have friends with a different skin color or differently shaped eyes.

It's not okay to judge people on their skin color or the shape of their eyes, only on what they do.

It's never okay to hurt someone else deliberately.

It's okay to hurt someone accidentally, because that means you had no control over it.

It's okay to tell someone not to do something bad.

It's okay to read the Bible. It's okay for someone else to read the Koran or the Bhagavad-gita.

It's okay for a friend to have a different religion.

It's okay to go to church. It's okay not to go to church.

It's okay to want your own job rather than what your parents had planned for you.

It's okay to want your kids to come home by a certain hour.

It's okay to want your kids to study hard.

It's okay to be grumpy sometimes. Everybody is grumpy sometimes.

It's okay to go jogging in the rain.

It's okay to rent a house, even if you can afford to buy.

It's okay to buy a house if you can afford it.

It's okay to buy used furniture.

It's okay to have pimples. Look around. You're not the only one.

It's okay to smile when you have braces. You'll be surprised that most people think it's cute.

It's okay to get shots if you need them. You'll discover that they don't hurt as much as you imagine.

It's okay to be afraid of heights. It's okay to figure out why you are afraid.

It's okay to be afraid of dogs. Some dogs are vicious. But it's okay to try to pet a friend's dog that you know to be gentle.

It's okay to want to travel to places where other people say they would not want to go.

It's okay to make a fool of yourself now and then.
It keeps you humble.

It's okay to take breaks during the day. Abraham Lincoln told a story about two men chopping wood. After awhile, one of them stopped chopping and disappeared. The other kept going, confident that he was going to chop the most wood that day. His friend came back and chopped some more, then disappeared again.

The first man noticed that his friend's woodpile was bigger than his, so he chopped even harder. At the end of the day, his friend's woodpile was twice as big as his. "What's the deal?" he asked his friend. "I've been chopping and chopping all day without a break, and you disappear every hour on the hour, and yet your woodpile is twice as big as mine. What were you doing when you quit chopping to go off somewhere?"

"Sharpening my axe," said his friend.

Taking breaks during the day lets you sharpen your axe so you can get more work done than you might otherwise.

It's okay not to achieve
everything you've ever
wanted to achieve.

It's okay for someone
else not to achieve some-
thing they've said they
would achieve. You don't
know everything that's
going on in their life.

It's okay not to be a mil-
lionaire by the time
you're 30.

It's okay to be sad.

It's okay to be sad if you lose a friend.

It's okay to be sad if you lose a member of your family.

It's okay to be sad if you lose your job.

It's okay to be sad if you have a bad day.

It's okay to be sad if someone makes fun of you. But that doesn't mean they're right.

It's okay to be sad if someone yells at you. But it's also okay to forget about it and be happy instead.

It's okay to be sad when others are happy.

It's okay to be happy when others are sad.

It's okay to be shorter than your friends.

It's okay to be taller than your friends.

It's okay to be fat, if you're not endangering your health or furniture.

It's okay to go on a diet, if you also begin to exercise. Exercise includes things you don't even think of as exercise, like walking up stairs.

It's okay to have a glass of wine with dinner. That doesn't make you an alcoholic. A wineglass holds four ounces, though, not forty-eight.

It's okay to be excited about a great idea.

It's okay to be excited about something good that happened to you.

It's okay for something good to happen to a friend when nothing good seems to happen to you. You might be overlooking something.

It's okay for something good to happen to someone you don't like. Remember, someone else might not like you. Does that mean nothing good should happen to you?

It's okay to have messy handwriting, but it's not okay to get mad if someone else can't read it.

It's okay to have a candy bar sometimes.
But not ten candy bars.

It's okay to mumble if you're shy, but no one will understand what you're saying and that will only make you feel more shy.

It's okay to ask a charity where your money goes. If they won't answer or it sounds suspicious, it's okay not to give them any money.

It's okay to invest in a stock that you think will go up.

It's okay for a stock to go down.

It's okay to sell a stock at a loss if you need the money right now.

It's okay to read a book instead of watching TV.

It's okay to go to a movie that you really want to see.

It's okay to go to a movie by yourself.

It's okay to do something nice for an older person. Offer them your seat, shovel their snow, mow their lawn, bring them a nice, home-cooked meal.

It's okay for someone to get cancer. Maybe there will be a cure someday.

It's okay for someone to get old. There's no escape. We all have to live with it. It's okay for someone to become senile. That happens.

It's okay to get wrinkles. Wrinkly people have done a lot of wonderful things.

It's okay to exercise if you have arthritis. Doctors even say it's good for you.

It's okay to wonder if a doctor is right. It's okay to ask for a second opinion, or a third.

It's okay to feel as if you're not getting the breaks others do. But look at someone like Jack Tramiel, who survived a Nazi concentration camp, and went on to build a huge computer company. When he was in the concentration camp, almost anybody else in the world was better off. But he survived. And ended up more successful than most people. Then he got booted out of his own computer company. And bought out another one. Lots of people hate him. Is he really successful? Who knows? But if someone can go through the hell of a concentration camp and do what Jack Tramiel did, can your life right now be truly hopeless?

It's okay to feel hopeless. For a little while. But then you should look at the good things that have happened to you, no matter how paltry they seem to be. There are probably more than you think.

It's okay to grow apart from friends. Everyone gets new interests. People change. If you grow out of your favorite clothes, it doesn't mean they aren't nice anymore, it just means they don't fit.

It's okay to feel as if you don't have any friends. But you probably do.

It's okay to worry about whether others have more friends than you. But do you like all their friends? Do they also have more *ex*-friends than you? Do you need that many friends?

It's okay to stay friends with an ex-boyfriend or ex-girlfriend or ex-spouse. You must have liked them before. Why do you have to stop liking them just because you're no longer dating them or living with them?

It's okay to disagree with friends about issues and still remain friends.

It's okay for you to write in your own book, tear out pages, cut out pictures. Books are made to be used. But it's not okay to do that to a library book or anybody else's book.

It's okay to feel that you look better than what you see in the mirror.

It's okay to look in the mirror and be disappointed with what you see. But what you see is what you get, and you either have to make the changes you can, or be happy with what you've got.

It's okay to be average.

It's okay to be aimless sometimes. But if you don't know where you're going, you'll never get there.

It's okay to have green hair and a ring in your nose.

It's okay for people to stare at you if you have green hair and a ring in your nose. Isn't that what you want?

It's okay to like chicken soup when you have a cold.

It's okay to drink water instead of soda pop. It's okay to have soda pop, though, if that's what you want.

It's okay to admit that you're wrong about something.

It's okay to point out when someone else is wrong. But do it in a way that's not insulting. Does it make you feel good to make them feel bad?

It's okay to take the time to think about what you're saying before you answer a question, unless you're on a game show.

It's okay to run out of cash at a restaurant. You can probably find some way to pay the bill. It's not okay to run out of a restaurant without paying the bill.

It's okay to be at a fancy restaurant and not know what all the silverware is for. Just ask someone. That shows you're smart, not dumb.

It's okay to hope you win a million dollars from Publisher's Clearinghouse.

It's okay not to win a million dollars from Publisher's Clearinghouse.

It's okay to go jogging in the rain.

It's okay to have grown up in another country.

It's okay to fight city hall. You're a citizen.

It's okay to like paying taxes. You owe it to your country.

It's okay to work at something you really love. If other people really care about you, they wouldn't complain about you doing what you love. But it's okay for them to worry about whether you're going to keep food on the table.

It's okay to be proud of something you've done well. It's okay for someone else to be proud of something they've done well.

It's okay to go to the racetrack. It's not okay to spend all your family's money at the racetrack. It's stupid.

It's okay to take a risk if you think it will pay off. But have a plan in case it doesn't.

It's okay to have grown up in poverty.

It's okay to have grown up fabulously wealthy.

It's okay to wear cheap tennis shoes.

It's okay to wear a cheap watch. Watches are for telling time, not for impressing people.

It's okay to wear goofy-looking clothes. In a few years, you might find out that goofy-looking clothes are fashionable, and what was fashionable, now looks goofy. Who'd have thought bell-bottoms and platform shoes would come back?

It's okay to forget to do something you promised to do, but only if you don't hurt anyone, and only if you don't do it very often.

It's not okay to cheat.

It's not okay to lie.

It's not okay to give your company's money and goods to friends without permission.

It's okay to believe in better living through chemistry. It's okay to criticize chemical companies for dumping toxic chemicals unsafely.

It's okay to believe in a better tomorrow.

It's okay to look for
the silver lining.

It's okay to tell your parents you love them.

It's okay to tell your children you love them.

It's okay to tell friends you love them. If they react as if you poured green slime all over them, at least they know how you feel about them.

It's okay not to tell your friends you love them. You probably already show it.

It's okay to vote for someone even if you think they might lose.

It's okay to belong to the other party. It's okay not to belong to any party.

It's okay to think that Herbert Hoover was a good president.

It's okay to think that Lyndon Johnson was a good president.

It's okay to think that Richard Nixon was a good president.

It's okay to think that Jimmy Carter was a good president.

It's okay to think that Ronald Reagan was a good president.

It's okay for other people to think otherwise.

It's okay to make jokes about the president.

It's okay for someone to live in America and criticize it.

It's okay to criticize the government for its conduct of a war. That's your prerogative as a citizen.

It's okay to defend America.

It's okay to have someone else look over your work.

It's okay for someone to criticize your work. Maybe they're right. Maybe they don't know what they're talking about.

It's okay to get mad at drivers who cut you off. It's not okay to get even. They probably didn't know they were cutting you off.

It's okay to use the "passenger's brake" if the person driving seems about to hit another car and you're scared for your life.

It's okay for the passenger to point out an oncoming car that the driver might not have seen.

It's okay for the driver to say, "Who's the driver here, anyway?"

It's okay to do something without your friends if they won't do it with you.

It's okay to believe you're thin.

It's okay to believe you don't look old.

It's okay to have saddlebags.

It's okay not to have any kids when you're 35.

It's okay to have four kids when you're just 30.

It's okay not to want to have kids. It's okay to change your mind.

It's okay not to be married when you thought you'd be married.

It's okay to ride the bus.

It's okay to ride your bike.

It's okay to ride the train.

It's okay to go to work by a different route.

It's okay to go to a public school.

It's okay to go to a private school.

It's okay to look at someone you love and smile.

It's okay to ask for help.

It's okay to turn 30.

It's okay to turn 40.

It's okay to turn 50.

If you're over 50, you already know it's okay to get older.

It's okay to wear your hair the same way you did in high school. But you should be aware that others might think it looks kind of funny.

It's okay not to know the answer.

It's okay to know most or all of the answers.

It's okay to ask questions when you don't know the answer.

It's okay to get the best score on a test.

It's okay to get the worst score on the test, but you shouldn't be proud of it.

It's okay to feel bad because you got the worst score on a test. Study more carefully and it won't ever happen again.

It's okay to feel bitter if you lose your job. But you won't find another job very fast by showing everyone how bitter you are.

It's okay for a woman to be a manager. It's okay for a woman to be president of a company. It's okay for a woman to be president of the country.

It's okay to know that your boss is wrong about something.
Nobody's perfect, even bosses.

It's okay to clean your kids' rooms, but ask yourself how many moms threw away their kids' stupid comic book collections, only to find out that this year those same comic books could pay for an entire college education.

It's okay to read comic books. At least you're reading.

It's okay to read science fiction.

It's okay to read science books that other people think are boring. Bill Gates is a billionaire because he did that.

It's okay to accidentally leave your fly open now and then. Bill Gates did, and look where he is today.

It's okay to have dandruff.

It's okay to grow a beard,
even if you really can't.

It's okay for people to think
you look scruffy if you
have a scraggly beard.

If you don't want people to
think you look scruffy,
shave your scraggly beard.

It's okay to hug someone you love.

It's okay not to like being hugged.

It's okay to have a bad dream.

It's okay to throw things away (or give them away), if they've been sitting around for years gathering dust in case they might be useful "someday."

It's okay to buy something new, even if you know you kept the old version around somewhere. You'll probably never find it. It's okay to look first.

It's okay to wait to buy something expensive.

It's okay to buy something expensive that you really don't need, as long as you can really afford it. But if you can't afford it, think twice. Then don't buy it.

It's okay to treat yourself if you have something to celebrate.

It's okay to celebrate when something good happens.

It's okay to treat yourself when you're feeling down, if that will lift your spirits.

It's okay, if you're knocked down, to get up and keep going.

It's okay to do something nice for your birthday.

It's okay if you don't want anyone to know your birthdate.

It's okay to grow long, narrow sideburns. It's okay for people to think they look doofy.

It's okay to rely on other people. If they turn out to be unreliable, that's a lesson for you both. If you know they're unreliable, you can't rely on them as heavily as you could if you knew they were reliable.

It's okay to feel good about advantages you have that others don't. If you can see, you can feel good about not being blind. If you're blind, you can feel good about not being deaf. If you're blind and deaf, then you're in the same position as Helen Keller, one of the most successful people of all time. Compared to her, what have you got to gripe about?

It's okay to do something incredibly stupid. It's probably the most stupid thing that anybody's ever done in the whole history of the world, but you'll get over it.

It's okay, if you're sad, to read a funny book or watch a funny movie.

It's okay, if you're sad, to read a sad book or watch a sad movie.

It's okay not to know how to cook.
It's okay to call someone and ask how to cook a hamburger.
It's okay to just heat frozen dinners.

It's okay to worry about winning a game. It's easier to win if you keep your eye on the ball instead of worrying about winning.

It's okay to lose a game. It's just a game. That's the neat thing about games. There will always be more games.

It's okay to win a game, even if you beat your friends at it. It's just a game.

It's okay for your team to lose the Super Bowl. They haven't let you down. They just lost a game. And they got paid a lot of money to play it.

It's okay to say ain't. But there ain't nothing wrong with sounding educated, either.

It's okay to work in a beauty shop.

It's okay to be a geologist.

It's okay to believe in crystals.

It's okay not to believe in crystals.

If you believe in crystals, it's okay to ask yourself whether you used to believe in est, TM, the guru Shree Rajneesh, Jim Jones, pyramid power, or Lifespring.

It's okay to be afraid. Often you'll find that there was nothing to be afraid of. And if there is something to be afraid of then you'll be able to handle it better if you're careful.

It's okay to go see a movie that turns out to be terrible. If it's so bad, you can just walk out. And you can probably get your money back.

It's okay to ask someone for change for a dollar bill if a vending machine won't take dollar bills.

It's okay to ask passersby for help if you need to catch a bus but find you don't have any money.

It's okay to help out someone who's short of bus money.

It's okay to get sick. You'll probably get well.

If you're sick, it's okay not to be able to get well. You wouldn't have planned it that way, but there's not a lot you can do about it. Why blame yourself?

It's okay not to go to the doctor for every little thing.

It's okay to go to the doctor if you need to.

It's okay not to go to the dentist every six months.

It's okay to go to the dentist before your teeth are visibly crumbling. In fact, it will save you money—and teeth.

It's okay to be in a wheelchair.

It's okay not to know a foreign language. But why be proud of that fact?

It's okay to want the best. If you don't try to be the best, to do the best, what are you trying for?

It's okay to not be the best. Just keep trying. Don't forget that the worst you can be is the best at being the worst.

Sometimes you get tired of doing things the same old way all the time. That's all right.

It's okay to be a complete slob. Just don't be surprised if people get disgusted at having to lift up an old banana peel or a smelly shirt every time they want to sit down. Don't be surprised if your friends don't like to come over to your place.

It's okay to be compulsive about cleaning your house.

Just don't be surprised if people get upset at not being allowed to sit on perfectly good furniture just because you're saving it for an important occasion.

Don't be surprised if your friends don't like to come over to your place.

It's okay for handicapped people to have handicapped parking spaces. If you were in a wheelchair, you'd appreciate the convenience.

It's not okay to park in a handicapped space, unless you're handicapped. Even if your car is new. Even if your car is expensive. Even if you're in a hurry. Even if you're important.

It's okay to feel guilty. That means that you know you did something wrong. It's okay to correct what you are doing wrong. Then you won't need to feel guilty.

It's okay to practice before you do something.

It's okay to study before you learn something.

It's okay to do homework, whether you're in school or in a job, if that's what it takes to do better.

It's okay to go to college.

It's okay not to go to college if you're not going to get anything out if it. You can always go back later.

It's okay to end up doing something you didn't originally plan on doing. Do you think someone actually plans to write a book like this?

It's okay to make your dog sleep outside.

It's okay to let your dog sleep inside.

It's okay to let your dog sleep on your bed, if you really feel like it and you don't mind hair all over your blankets, but only if the person who cleans the blankets agrees.

It's okay to pray if you believe.

It's okay to pray if you don't believe.

It's okay not to pray whether or not you believe.

It's okay to pray for something for yourself.

It's okay to pray for an end to war, an end to starvation, an end to violence, and to pray that everyone on earth will be able to live a safe, comfortable, and fulfilling life, and since *you're* on earth, that prayer includes you, too.

It's okay to oppose something you know is wrong.

It's okay for others to disagree with you. It's okay to try to convince them otherwise. It's okay if you can't convince them.

It's okay to split the bill with friends at the restaurant. It's best to decide how you're going to split the bill before you order, though.

It's okay for your boss to fire you if you're always late for work.

It's okay to stay up late if you don't feel sleepy, as long as you can get up when you have to the next morning.

It's okay to go to bed early, if that works better for you.

It's okay to toss and turn all night long. You won't do that every night. It means you were thinking about something.

It's okay to get up and read, if you're tossing and turning and having trouble sleeping.

It's okay to sleep in when you have nothing important to do.

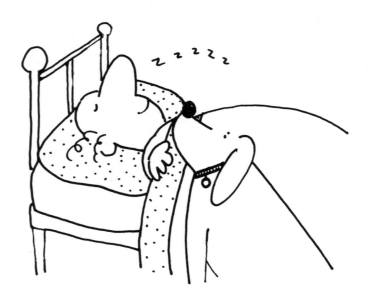

It's okay to think unhappy thoughts. Just recognize them as thoughts, not reality. And remember that you're allowed to have happy thoughts, too.

It's okay to blame others for things if you know they're responsible, but isn't it better to try to make right whatever was done wrong?

It's okay to blame your parents for your own problems, like drug addiction, child-beating, spousal abuse, but it's up to you to solve them.

It's okay to be part of the problem, because then you might have a better idea of how to be part of the solution.

It's okay not to give up.

It's okay to keep on trying.

It's okay to know when to quit. Quitting is not the same as giving up.

It's okay not to want to meet someone you think you might not like. It's okay to meet them anyway. You might find you like them.

It's okay to dread getting together with a friend's friends. They may dread meeting you. They may become your friends.

It's okay not to like your friend's friends. Or your wife's friends. Or your husband's friends. But that doesn't mean you don't have to get along with them.

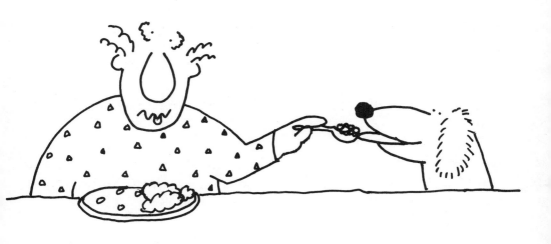

It's okay to dislike certain kinds of food.

It's okay to try foods you've never tried before.

It's okay to eat meatloaf.

It's okay to eat out if you hate cooking and you can afford it.

It's okay to eat at home all the time because you can't afford to go out.

It's okay to try something new. It's okay to flub up the first time you try it. And the next time. And the next time. You're not failing, you're learning.

It's okay to be depressed. You wouldn't be depressed if something weren't seriously wrong. But it's okay to get better, too. And it's okay to get better fast.

It's okay to hire someone to do your housework, if you can afford it.

It's okay to do your own housework, whether or not you can afford it.

It's okay to be a teacher.

It's okay to be a student.

It's okay to have big dreams for yourself. But let others dream their own dreams. If you want them to follow your dream, you have to show them how to make it their dream, too.

It's okay to have little dreams for yourself. But don't stop others from having big dreams.

It's okay to save money so that you can buy something later.

It's okay to buy something that you've been saving for, once you have saved enough to afford it.

It's okay not to buy something you've been saving for if you decide you don't really need it.

It's okay to let money just sit in a savings account if you don't need it right now.

It's okay not to spend money if you don't need to.

It's okay to let other people succeed.

It's okay for you to succeed.

It's okay to have holes in your underwear.

It's okay to make piles of money on Wall Street. It's not okay to do it by cheating, lying, stealing, or misrepresenting what you know to be the truth.

It's okay to work at a low-paying job for a nonprofit organization you believe in.

It's okay for you to think you can, think you can, think you can. Because you know you can.

It's okay to watch violent movies. It's not okay to be violent.

It's okay to watch syruppy movies.

It's okay to cry at movies, preferably at sad moments.

It's okay to help someone else do better.

It's okay to share if you have enough.

It's okay to share if you don't have enough.

It's okay not to share if you don't have enough.

It's okay to talk to someone you're mad at. Sometimes that's the best possible thing to do.

It's okay not to want to talk to someone you're mad at. But if they try to talk to you, then you should give them the benefit of the doubt and try to patch things up. If you end up in a shouting match, well, at least you tried to make things right.

It's okay to put things off.

It's okay to be yelled at for putting things off too long.

It's okay to finish something you've put off for a long time.

It's okay to get started on something you've put off for a long time, even if you think you can't finish it.

It's okay to wear glasses.

It's okay to hate wearing glasses.

It's okay to break a glass by accident.

It's okay to spill your milk by accident.

It's okay to prefer the company of animals to the company of humans. But ask yourself why you really feel that way. Maybe you're nicer to animals than you are to humans.

It's okay to judge others, but realize that your judgment might be faulty.

It's okay to be a debater. It's okay to be a master debater.

It's okay to write a letter to someone you should have written to long ago.

It's okay to want to be popular. If you're likeable, it's easier to be popular.

It's okay to feel unpopular. Some of the most popular people feel unpopular.

It's okay to say that life isn't a popularity contest.

It's okay to feel that it is.

It's okay not to care whether life is a popularity contest.

It's okay to want to be liked. It's easier to be liked if you make yourself likeable.

It's okay to believe in yourself.

It's okay to stop getting mad at the little things someone does that always annoy you. It's okay to tell that person what it is they do that annoys you.

It's okay to overcome overwhelming odds.

When you're down, when things couldn't be bleaker, it's okay to aim for victory.

It's okay to treat yourself now and then.

It's okay to relax.

It's okay to take time to stretch in the middle of the day.

It's okay to take time off.

It's okay to take a vacation.

It's okay to be chubbier
than your siblings.

It's okay to be thinner
than your siblings.

It's okay to be taller
than your siblings.

It's okay to be shorter
than your siblings.

It's okay to have a name that could be either a man's or a woman's name. You can use another name if you don't like it.

It's okay to be a salesman. It's not okay to lie or cheat. Most salesmen don't need to do that.

It's okay for men to wear gold chains.

It's okay to think that gold chains are kind of sleazy.

It's okay to gain a few pounds. You'll probably lose them.

It's okay to skip your exercise program for today, whether you're too busy or just don't feel like it—but an exercise program isn't much good if you never do it.

It's okay to run that extra mile if you're in good shape and want to go for it.

It's okay to try and lift a higher weight—if you can't lift it comfortably, at least you tried. You'll be able to do it soon enough.

It's okay to do an okay job.

It's okay to be the best at something.

It's okay not to be the best at something. It's even okay to be the worst at something. You're not the worst at everything, and you're probably the best at something else.

It's okay not to be the best at anything. Just do your best.

It's okay to work really hard for something and then not get what you want. How do you know that getting it would really have been the best thing for you?

It's okay to ask other people about themselves. It's okay for other people to ask about yourself. They're probably interested in you.

It's okay to be Italian.

It's okay to be French.

It's okay to be Chinese.

It's okay to be Zulu.

It's okay to be Tatar.

It's okay to be Algonquin.

It's okay to be Maori.

It's okay to be an aboriginal Australian.

It's okay to be Christian.

It's okay to be Hindu.

It's okay to be Muslim.

It's okay to be Serbian.

It's okay to be Croatian.

It's okay to be Armenian.

It's okay to be Turkish.

It's okay to be Greek.

It's okay to be any race, creed, or color. If you make a habit of hating other people because of the way they look or dress or speak, don't forget that they can hate you for equally worthless reasons. Why would you want to be hated?

It's okay to marry someone who is not of your "class." How much class do you have if you base marriage on financial status? Love is more important than money.

If you're poor, it's okay to marry someone who's rich.

If you're rich, it's okay to marry someone who's poor.

It's okay to marry someone who's rich, even if you don't really love them, because they really want to marry you—as long as you treat them the way you would treat someone you loved.

It's okay to thank someone.

It's okay to be thanked.

It's okay to ask someone to repeat their name or to spell it for you.

It's okay to forget someone's name. Tell them nicely that you forgot.

It's okay to tell someone your troubles.

It's okay to listen to someone telling you their troubles.

It's okay not to listen to someone's troubles, but you should be sympathetic; they need a shoulder to cry on, not a cold shoulder. If you don't feel you can give them a shoulder to cry on, you can still be nice to them.

It's okay to ask someone to repeat a question or an answer.

It's okay for a charity to ask for money.

It's okay for you not to give a charity money.

It's okay to let the answering machine answer phone solicitations. You're never obligated to answer the phone just because it rings. The telemarketers are counting on you being nice. Are they being nice to interrupt your day?

It's okay to count to ten before you yell at anyone.
Then it's okay not to yell at them.

It's okay for a collection agency to try to collect on an overdue bill. That's their job. They're not your enemy.

It's okay to ask a collection agency if there's some way to pay off your debt slowly, if you can't afford to pay it all at once.

It's okay to pay off all your credit card charges every month.

It's okay to pause in the middle of a sentence if you're trying to find the right words.

It's okay to pause in the middle of a sentence if you forgot what you were saying. It's okay to tell someone that you forgot what you were saying.

It's okay to speak in plain English, even if you're a college professor or a computer programmer.

It's okay to write the way you talk. There's no law that says writing has to sound pompous and overly complicated.

It's okay to use big words, if you're willing to explain what they mean to people who don't know.

It's okay to be in a bad mood, but don't wonder why people aren't being nice to you at that time.

It's okay for someone else to be in a good mood when you're in a bad mood.

It's okay to be yourself. Make sure you're being yourself, though, and not someone else's idea of yourself.

It's okay to be concerned about what happens to people you don't really know.

It's okay to work at McDonald's. You don't have to stay there forever, and you don't know where the opportunity might lead.

It's okay to be a priest.

It's okay to work in a foundry.

It's okay to work in an ice-cream parlor.

It's okay to be a garbage collector.

It's okay to be a janitor.

It's okay to whistle
while you work.

It's okay to get a college degree.

It's okay to go to graduate school, if you really want to study a subject in depth or specialize in it.

It's okay to get an MBA.

It's okay not to get an MBA.

It's okay not to trust people with MBAs.

It's okay to be a lawyer. Lawyers are actually necessary.

It's okay to think that some lawyers are not interested in justice.

It's okay to think that some doctors are not interested in helping heal the sick.

It's okay to ask for several doctors' opinions before undergoing a heart-bypass operation.

It's okay to ask for second opinions before having any surgery.

It's okay to have cosmetic surgery. It's okay to donate the money to the poor instead.

It's okay to ask for several doctors' opinions before undergoing a caesarian section.

It's okay to use a midwife to deliver a baby during a normal pregnancy, where it's legal. It's not legal in some states.

It's okay to prefer to deliver your baby in the hospital.

It's okay to say "Goodbye" before you hang up the phone.

It's okay to say, "I'm sorry, I must have dialed the wrong number," if you've dialed a wrong number.

It is okay to say, "Have a nice day." But don't expect everyone to want to have a nice day.

It's okay not to be businesslike. What does it mean to be "businesslike" anyway?

It's okay to listen to criticism.

It's okay to offer constructive criticism. Make sure it's constructive.

It's okay to have greasy and dirty hair, but wouldn't it feel less itchy if you washed it more often?

It's okay to wear your hair so that it looks greasy and dirty, if that's how you want it to look.

It's okay to get a pilot's license when you're sixty-four.

It's okay to get a college degree when you're seventy.

It's okay to learn to read when you're a hundred and three.

It's okay to teach an old dog new tricks.

It's okay to treat customers like human beings.

It's okay to treat salespeople and staff members like human beings.

It's okay to get seasick.

It's okay to take seasick pills if you're a guy.

It's okay to wear one of those goofy wristbands with a marble in it that presses on some nerve to combat motion sickness. They really are supposed to work.

It's okay to feel faint if you stand up too fast. You're probably not having a heart attack.

It's okay to take medicine your doctor prescribes. If you think the doctor is overprescribing, you can talk to another doctor.

It's okay to listen to records when you're feeling down. Or play the piano. Or go for a run. Or go see a movie.

It's okay to cover your mouth when you cough or sneeze.

It's okay to wear a hat when it's cold.

It's okay to wear boots when it's nasty outside.

It's okay to wear a Hawaiian shirt to the office.

It's okay for your boss to complain if you wear a Hawaiian shirt to the office.

It's okay to quit your job. It's okay to have a new job lined up first.

It's okay to be afraid of lightning.

It's okay to pick up hitchhikers.

It's okay not to pick up hitchhikers.

It's okay to stop and help out someone stranded by the side of the road. It's sad that anyone in this country should be worried that someone who seems stranded by the side of the road might be dangerous. It's sad that anyone dangerous would pretend to be stranded by the side of the road, because that hurts every single other person who is ever really going to be stranded by the side of the road.

It's okay to call the police if you see a problem along the road.

It's okay to report a crime you witnessed. In fact, it's imperative.

If someone is being very hard on you, it's okay to love that person. It's also okay to say, "Forget this, man, I'm outta here!"

It's okay to grovel. But ask yourself why you would bother.

It's okay to hum when you're happy.

It's okay to hum when you're sad.

It's okay to start fresh every day.

It's okay to want something for nothing.

It's okay not to get something for nothing.

It's okay not to win a contest.

It's okay to love high, craggy, ocean cliffs.

It's okay to love the fog.

It's okay to love the snow.

It's okay to drive across the lines of an empty parking lot.

It's okay to walk against a red light at three in the morning if nobody's coming.

It's okay for a policemen who happens to see you cross against a red light at three in the morning to give you a ticket for jay-walking.

It's okay to love sandy beaches.

It's okay to love warm sunshine.

It's okay to lay out in the sun.

It's okay to prevent skin cancer.

It's okay to meditate.

It's okay for people to ride their bikes in the bike lane. It's okay for them to ride on the side of a road without a bike lane.

It's okay to be perturbed if someone on a bike darts out in front of your car.

It's okay to Walk in the Path of Righteousness. But don't assume you're the only one walking there.

It's okay to turn the other cheek.

It's okay not to hit back.

It's okay not to hit first.

It's okay not to hit.

It's okay to defend yourself. That doesn't mean you have to injure someone else. If the option's available, running away and screaming are means of self-defense, too.

It's okay to prepare yourself for self-defense. Try something non-aggressive like aikido, instead of buying a gun. Consider that most victims of handguns are family members and friends, not burglars and rapists.

It's okay to want to put professional criminals behind bars.

It's okay to want to reform professional criminals.

It's okay to try to give an ex-con a second chance.

It's okay to demand restitution from thieves.

It's okay to think that vicious killers deserve the death penalty.

It's okay to think that "Thou shalt not kill" includes us as well as murderers.

It's okay to oppose war. It's okay to work at preventing war.

It's okay to support a war for a just cause.

It's okay to be a conscientious objector.

It's okay to visit people in an old-folks home. It's okay to call it an old-folks home. It's filled with old folks.

It's okay to send a birthday card to someone you love.

It's okay for someone to die when you don't expect it. That happens.

It's okay to cook a meal for a family that's grieving.

It's okay to give food to the poor.

It's okay to give money to a bum. Maybe someday you'll be a bum. Not all bums are drunks. Even drunks have to eat.

It's okay for you to think that you're the only person who ever had to go through whatever you're going through. It's okay for others to suggest that you're not the only one.

It's okay to blame others for your problems. It's okay to wonder if maybe you might be partly at fault. Or completely at fault.

It's okay to let your children live their own lives.

It's okay to let your parents live their own lives.

It's okay to live with your parents after you graduate from high school.

It's okay for your parents to kick you out after you graduate from high school.

If you're living at home, it's okay for your parents to ask you to help out around the house and keep your room clean.

It's okay for you to want some privacy.

It's okay to enjoy your job. It's okay to have a job you enjoy.

It's okay to rest when you're sick.

It's okay to rest when you're recovering from surgery.

It's okay to try and get moving as soon as you can after you had surgery. It's okay to rest some more if it hurts too much to get moving.

It's okay to get discouraged. It's also okay to keep moving forward.

It's okay to search for hidden treasure. Just don't get lost.

It's okay to plan for the future.

It's okay not to know how to do something. Nobody knows how to do everything. Everyone had to learn everything they know.

It's okay to try to cheer somebody up.

It's okay to cheer somebody up with this book. Even yourself.

If you're unable to find additional copies of this book at your bookstore, it's okay to order them directly from the publisher at $5.95 each.

Yes! I would like more copies!   Quantity: _____

    Subtotal (multiply price by order quantity): _____

    California residents add 8.25% sales tax: _____

    Shipping and handling ($2.00 per copy): _____

                  Total cost: _____

Name _____

Address _____

City _____ State _____ Zip _____

Mail check or money order with a copy of this form to:

Tipperary Press
P.O. Box 9940
Stanford, CA 94309   (Please allow six to eight weeks for delivery.)

154

It's okay to like this book so much that you want to drop us a line! We're just a tiny company, trying to figure out what to do next. If you would like information about future products, like *It's Okay* t-shirts, calendars, or greeting cards, send us your name and address and we will add you to our mailing list. Our address is:

Tipperary Press
P.O. Box 9940
Stanford, California 94309

We'll be thrilled to hear from you!